ALL ABOARD!

PASSENGER TRAINS

by Nikki Bruno Clapper

Consulting Editor: Gail Saunders-Smith, PhD

Consultant: Martin Wachs, PhD,
Distinguished Professor Emeritus
of Urban Planning, UCLA

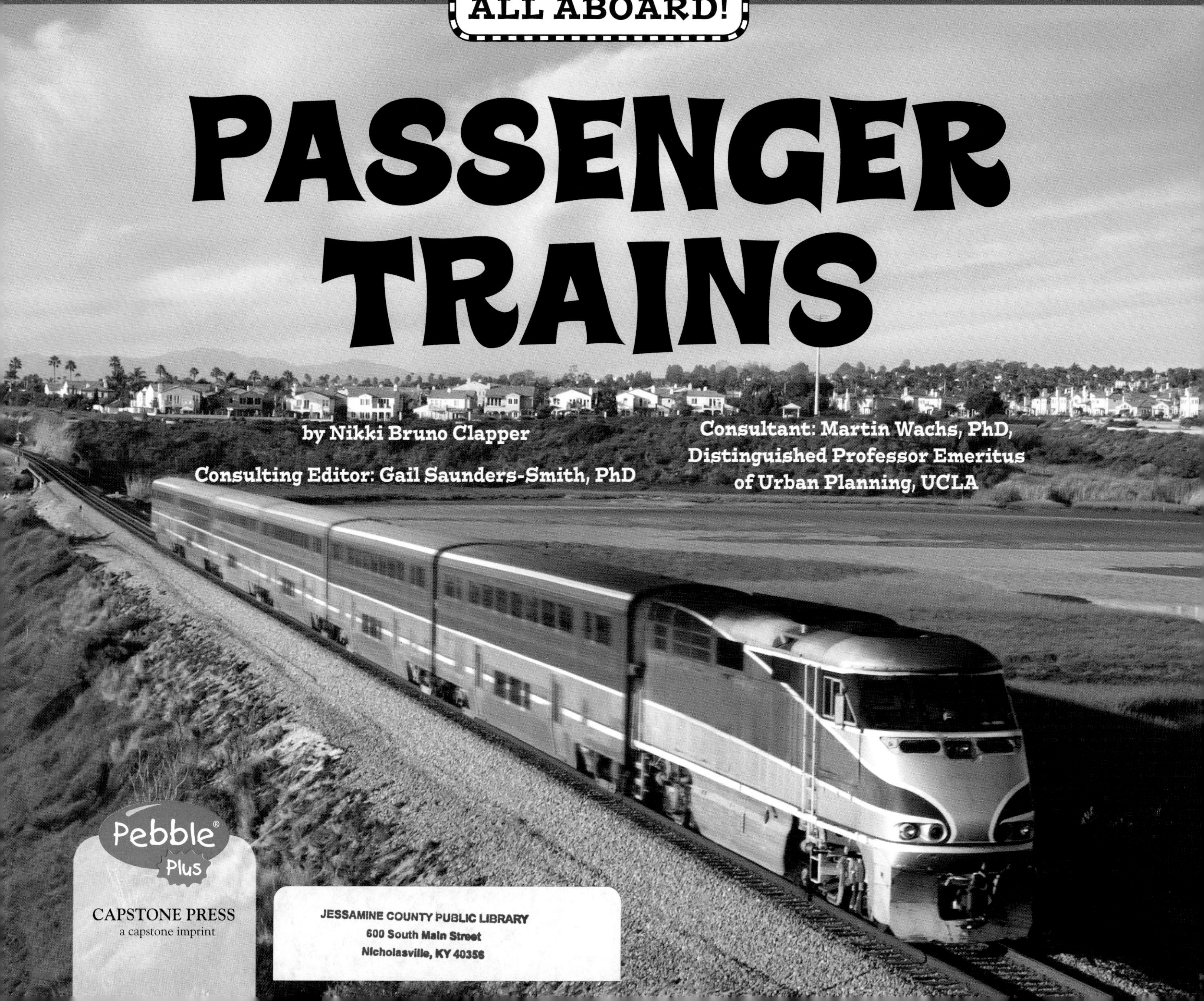

Pebble® Plus

CAPSTONE PRESS
a capstone imprint

Pebble Plus is published by Capstone Press,
1710 Roe Crest Drive, North Mankato, Minnesota 56003
www.capstonepub.com

Library of Congress Cataloging-in-Publication Data
Cataloging-in-publication data is on file with the Library of Congress.
ISBN 978-1-4914-6040-5 (library binding)
ISBN 978-1-4914-6060-3 (eBook PDF)

Editorial Credits
Nikki Bruno Clapper and Linda Staniford, editors; Juliette Peters, designer;
Jo Miller, media researcher; Kathy McColley, production specialist

Photo Credits
Alamy: Jim West, 19, P.Spiro, 9; Corbis: Walter Geiersperger, 11; Glow Images: Cultura RM/
Simon McComb, 17, SuperStock, 15; Newscom: Design Pics/Keith Levit, 7, Iter-Tass Photos/
Saverkin Alexander, 21, Westend61 GmbH/ImageINC, 13, ZUMA Press/Maisant Ludovic, 5;
Shutterstock: Eldad Carin, cover (ticket), Rostislav Glinsky, 2-3, 22-23, ShortPhotos, 1, topimages,
cover (train), tovovan, train design element, (throughout)

Note to Parents and Teachers

The All Aboard! set explores and supports the standard "Science, Technology, and Society," as required by the National Council for Social Studies. This book describes and illustrates passenger trains. The images support early readers in understanding the text. The repetition of words and phrases helps early readers learn new words. This book also introduces early readers to subject-specific vocabulary words, which are defined in the Glossary section. Early readers may need assistance to read some words and to use the Table of Contents, Glossary, Read More, Internet Sites, and Index sections of the book.

Printed in China by Nordica.
0415/CA21500542
032015   008837NORDF15

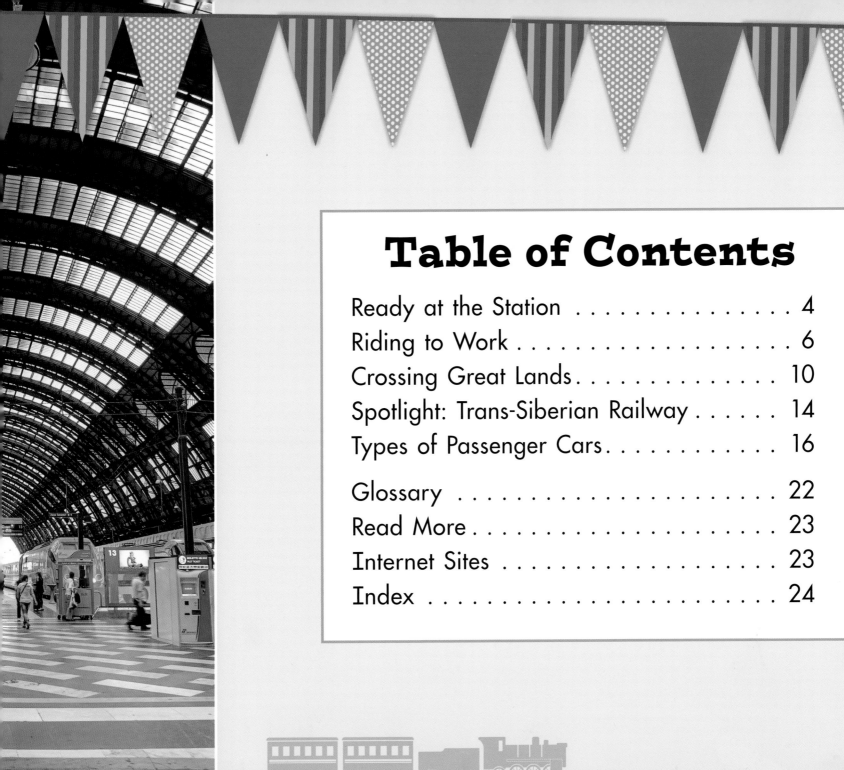

Table of Contents

Ready at the Station

The distant roar gets louder.

A warning bell rings.

The train screeches to a stop

at your feet. All aboard!

Riding to Work

Many people ride trains to and from work or school every day. These commuter trains connect suburbs to large cities.

Commuter trains are made
for medium-size trips.
Most people ride for less
than one hour. The trains
can get very crowded.

Crossing Great Lands

Long-distance trains can cross whole continents. Passengers ride for hours or even days. They look at beautiful scenery.

Comfort is important

on long-distance trains.

Large seats lean back.

There is a lot of leg space.

Most cars have restrooms.

Spotlight: Trans-Siberian Railway

The Trans-Siberian Railway

runs one of the world's longest

train rides. It takes seven

days to travel 6,000 miles

(9,656 kilometers) across Russia.

Types of Passenger Cars

Train cars differ by class.
First-class and business-class
cars are comfortable and
spacious. Coach-class cars
are less fancy.

a first-class train car

17

Train cars also differ by purpose. Dining cars serve food and drinks. These cars are important on long rides.

Some long-distance passenger trains have sleeper cars. These cars have beds for overnight trips.

GLOSSARY

business class—the second-highest class of service on a train or a plane

car—one of the wheeled vehicles that are put together to form a train

coach class—the most basic class of service on a train or a plane

commuter—a person traveling to work or school

connect—to join together two or more places

continent—one of Earth's seven large land masses

first class—the highest class of service on a train or a plane

luggage—suitcases, bags, and other containers for traveling

passenger—a person who rides on an airplane, train, or other vehicle

scenery—a view or landscape

suburb—a community near a city

READ MORE

Goodman, Susan E. *Trains! Step into Reading.* New York: Random House, 2012.

Shields, Amy. *Trains. National Geographic Readers.* Washington, D.C.: National Geographic, 2011.

INTERNET SITES

FactHound offers a safe, fun way to find Internet sites related to this book. All of the sites on FactHound have been researched by our staff.

Here's all you do:

Visit *www.facthound.com*

Type in this code: 9781491460405

Check out projects, games and lots more at
www.capstonekids.com

INDEX

Word Count: 174
Grade: 1
Early-Intervention Level: 18